Recipes to make your own gifts!

Use these recipes to delight your friends and family. Each recipe includes gift tags for your convenience — just cut them out and personalize. After personalizing your tag, attach it to the bottle using raffia, ribbon, twine or yarn.

Use a variety of different bottle sizes and shapes according to your tastes. Depending on the size of the recipe and bottles you use, you may be able to fill 1, 2 or even 3 bottles. Decorative bottles can be found at craft or import stores. (Or keep your eyes open at garage sales and flea markets!)

Copyright © 2004 CQ Products
Waverly, IA 50677
All right reserved.
No part of this book may be reproduced or transmitted
in any form or by any means, electronic or mechanical,
including photocopying, recording or by any information
storage and retrieval system, without permission in
writing from the publisher.

Printed in the United States of America
by G&R Publishing Co.

Distributed By:

507 Industrial Street
Waverly, IA 50677

ISBN 1-56383-170-8
Item # 3410

Romantic Bath Crystals

2 C. Epsom salts
10 drops rose essential oil
10 drops ylang ylang or sandalwood
   essential oil
5 drops red food coloring

In a medium bowl, combine Epsom salts, rose essential oil and ylang ylang or sandalwood essential oil. Mix well. Add drops of red food coloring and mix until well coated. Using a funnel, transfer to a decorative sealable bottle.

Attach a gift tag with directions on how to use bath crystals.

Gift Tag Directions:

Romantic Bath Crystals

Add 2 to 4 tablespoons Romantic Bath Crystals to warm running bath water. Soak, relax and enjoy!

Romantic Bath Crystals

Add 2 to 4 tablespoons Romantic Bath Crystals to warm running bath water. Soak, relax and enjoy!

Romantic Bath Crystals

Add 2 to 4 tablespoons Romantic Bath Crystals to warm running bath water. Soak, relax and enjoy!

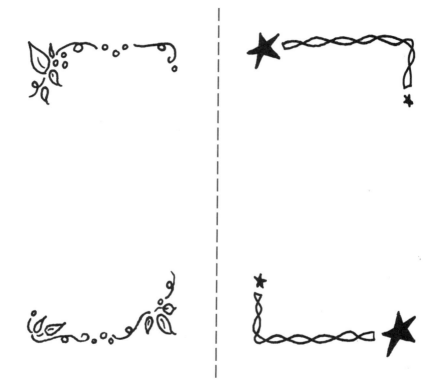

Romantic Bath Crystals

Add 2 to 4 tablespoons Romantic Bath Crystals to warm running bath water. Soak, relax and enjoy!

Romantic Bath Crystals

Add 2 to 4 tablespoons Romantic Bath Crystals to warm running bath water. Soak, relax and enjoy!

Grapefruit Bubble Bath

1/2 C. unscented shampoo
3/4 C. water
1/2 tsp. salt
10 drops grapefruit essential oil
Orange food coloring, optional

In a large bowl, place shampoo and water. Stir gently until well mixed. Add salt and stir until mixture thickens. Add grapefruit essential oil and mix well. If desired, add food coloring and mix until evenly incorporated. Using a funnel, transfer to a decorative sealable bottle.

Attach a gift tag with directions on how to use bubble bath.

Gift Tag Directions:

Grapefruit Bubble Bath

Add 2 to 4 tablespoons Grapefruit Bubble Bath to warm running bath water. Soak, relax and enjoy!

**Grapefruit
Bubble Bath**

Add 2 to 4 tablespoons Grapefruit Bubble Bath to warm running bath water. Soak, relax and enjoy!

**Grapefruit
Bubble Bath**

Add 2 to 4 tablespoons Grapefruit Bubble Bath to warm running bath water. Soak, relax and enjoy!

Grapefruit Bubble Bath

Add 2 to 4 tablespoons Grapefruit Bubble Bath to warm running bath water. Soak, relax and enjoy!

Grapefruit Bubble Bath

Add 2 to 4 tablespoons Grapefruit Bubble Bath to warm running bath water. Soak, relax and enjoy!

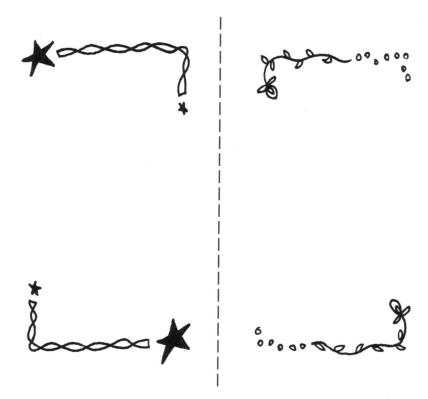

Muscle Relaxing Bath Salts

    2 C. Epsom salts or sea salts
    5 drops lavender essential oil
    3 drops blue food coloring, optional
    1/2 C. dried rose petals, optional

In a medium bowl, combine Epsom salts and lavender essential oil. Mix well. If desired, stir in blue food coloring and dried rose petals, until evenly incorporated. Using a funnel, transfer to a decorative sealable bottle.

Attach a gift tag with directions on how to use bath salts.

Gift Tag Directions:

Muscle Relaxing Bath Salts

Add 2 to 4 tablespoons Muscle Relaxing Bath Salts to warm running bath water. Soak, relax and enjoy!

Muscle Relaxing Bath Salts

Add 2 to 4 tablespoons Muscle Relaxing Bath Salts to warm running bath water. Soak, relax and enjoy!

Muscle Relaxing Bath Salts

Add 2 to 4 tablespoons Muscle Relaxing Bath Salts to warm running bath water. Soak, relax and enjoy!

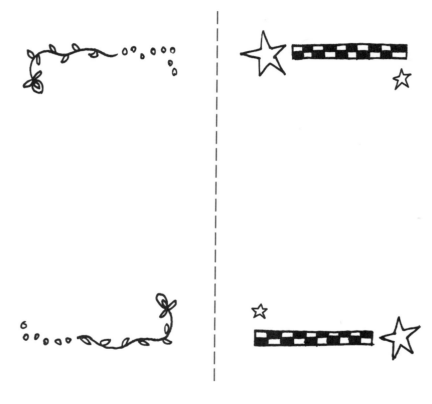

**Muscle Relaxing
Bath Salts**

Add 2 to 4
tablespoons Muscle
Relaxing Bath Salts
to warm running
bath water. Soak,
relax and enjoy!

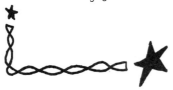

**Muscle Relaxing
Bath Salts**

Add 2 to 4
tablespoons Muscle
Relaxing Bath Salts
to warm running
bath water. Soak,
relax and enjoy!

Fairy Dust Glitter Gel

1/4 C. aloe vera gel
1 tsp. glycerin
1/4 tsp. polyester glitter
5 drops lavender essential oil, optional
Blue food coloring, optional

In a medium bowl, combine aloe vera gel and glycerin. Mix well and stir in glitter. If desired, add lavender essential oil and food coloring. Using a funnel, transfer to a decorative sealable bottle.

Attach a gift tag with directions on how to use glitter gel.

Gift Tag Directions:

Fairy Dust Glitter Gel

Massage a generous amount of Fairy Dust Glitter Gel into clean, dry skin for a shinning and glowing finish.

**Fairy Dust
Glitter Gel**

Massage a
generous amount of
Fairy Dust Glitter
Gel into clean, dry
skin for a shinning
and glowing finish.

**Fairy Dust
Glitter Gel**

Massage a
generous amount of
Fairy Dust Glitter
Gel into clean, dry
skin for a shinning
and glowing finish.

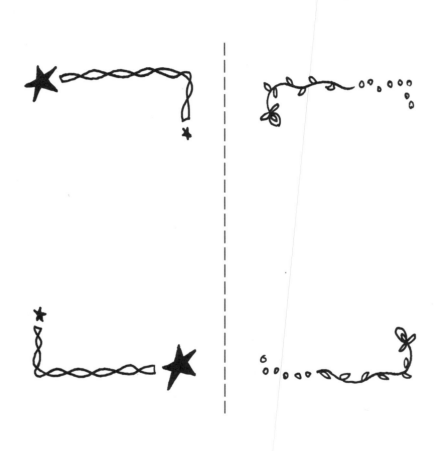

**Fairy Dust
Glitter Gel**

Massage a generous amount of Fairy Dust Glitter Gel into clean, dry skin for a shinning and glowing finish.

**Fairy Dust
Glitter Gel**

Massage a generous amount of Fairy Dust Glitter Gel into clean, dry skin for a shinning and glowing finish.

Skin So Soft Bath Soak

1 C. powdered milk
3 to 5 drops lavender or ylang ylang
    essential oil

In a medium bowl, combine powdered milk and lavender or ylang ylang essential oil. Mix until well blended. Using a funnel, transfer to a decorative sealable bottle.

Attach a gift tag with directions on how to use bath soak.

Gift Tag Directions:

Skin So Soft Bath Soak

Add a generous amount of Skin So Soft Bath Soak to warm running bath water. Soak, relax and enjoy!

Skin So Soft Bath Soak

Add a generous amount of Skin So Soft Bath Soak to warm running bath water. Soak, relax and enjoy!

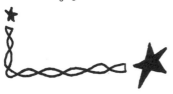

Skin So Soft Bath Soak

Add a generous amount of Skin So Soft Bath Soak to warm running bath water. Soak, relax and enjoy!

**Skin So Soft
Bath Soak**

Add a generous amount of Skin So Soft Bath Soak to warm running bath water. Soak, relax and enjoy!

**Skin So Soft
Bath Soak**

Add a generous amount of Skin So Soft Bath Soak to warm running bath water. Soak, relax and enjoy!

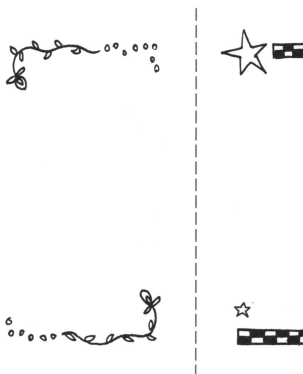

Oatmeal Milk Bath

1 C. cornstarch
2 C. powdered milk
1/2 C. oatmeal

Using a funnel, layer cornstarch, powdered milk and oatmeal into a decorative sealable bottle, one ingredient at a time. If desired, you can mix all ingredients together in a medium bowl before transferring to a decorative bottle.

Attach a gift tag with directions on how to use milk bath.

Gift Tag Directions:

Oatmeal Milk Bath

Add a generous amount of Oatmeal Milk Bath to warm running bath water. Soak, relax and enjoy!

Oatmeal Milk Bath

Add a generous amount of Oatmeal Milk Bath to warm running bath water. Soak, relax and enjoy!

Oatmeal Milk Bath

Add a generous amount of Oatmeal Milk Bath to warm running bath water. Soak, relax and enjoy!

Oatmeal Milk Bath

Add a generous amount of Oatmeal Milk Bath to warm running bath water. Soak, relax and enjoy!

Oatmeal Milk Bath

Add a generous amount of Oatmeal Milk Bath to warm running bath water. Soak, relax and enjoy!

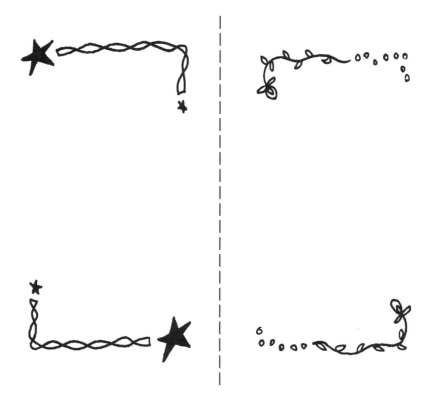

Soothing Rose Bath Crystals

1 C. Epsom salts
1 C. salt
1 C. baking soda
10 drops rose essential oil
Red food coloring, optional

In a large bowl, combine Epsom salts, salt and baking soda. Mix well. Add rose essential oil and mix until well combined. If desired, add food coloring and mix until evenly incorporated. Using a funnel, transfer to a decorative sealable bottle.

Attach a gift tag with directions on how to use bath crystals.

Gift Tag Directions:

Soothing Rose Bath Crystals

Add 2 to 4 tablespoons Soothing Rose Bath Crystals to warm running bath water. Soak, relax and enjoy!

Soothing Rose Bath Crystals

Add 2 to 4 tablespoons Soothing Rose Bath Crystals to warm running bath water. Soak, relax and enjoy!

Soothing Rose Bath Crystals

Add 2 to 4 tablespoons Soothing Rose Bath Crystals to warm running bath water. Soak, relax and enjoy!

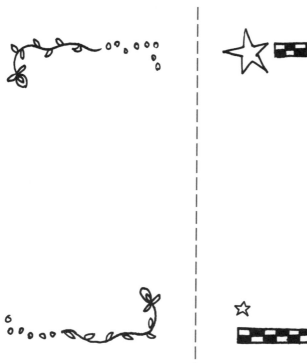

Soothing Rose Bath Crystals

Add 2 to 4 tablespoons Soothing Rose Bath Crystals to warm running bath water. Soak, relax and enjoy!

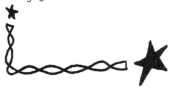

Soothing Rose Bath Crystals

Add 2 to 4 tablespoons Soothing Rose Bath Crystals to warm running bath water. Soak, relax and enjoy!

Lavender Dreams Bubble Bath

1/2 C. unscented shampoo
3/4 C. water
1/2 tsp. salt
15 drops lavender essential oil
Equal amounts of red and blue food coloring

In a large bowl, pour shampoo and add water. Stir gently until well mixed. Add salt and stir until mixture thickens. Add lavender essential oil and mix well. Add food coloring and mix until evenly incorporated. Using a funnel, transfer to a decorative sealable bottle.

Attach a gift tag with directions on how to use bubble bath.

Gift Tag Directions:

Lavender Dreams Bubble Bath

Add 2 to 4 tablespoons Lavender Dreams Bubble Bath to warm running bath water. Soak, relax and enjoy!

**Lavender Dreams
Bubble Bath**

Add 2 to 4 tablespoons Lavender Dreams Bubble Bath to warm running bath water. Soak, relax and enjoy!

**Lavender Dreams
Bubble Bath**

Add 2 to 4 tablespoons Lavender Dreams Bubble Bath to warm running bath water. Soak, relax and enjoy!

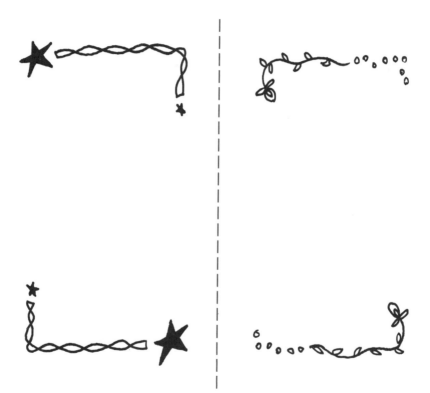

**Lavender Dreams
Bubble Bath**

Add 2 to 4 tablespoons Lavender Dreams Bubble Bath to warm running bath water. Soak, relax and enjoy!

**Lavender Dreams
Bubble Bath**

Add 2 to 4 tablespoons Lavender Dreams Bubble Bath to warm running bath water. Soak, relax and enjoy!

Soul Soothing Bath Salts

2 C. Epsom salts
1 C. sea salts
10 drops lavender essential oil
10 drops peppermint essential oil
Blue and green food coloring

In a large bowl, combine Epsom salts, sea salts, lavender essential oil and peppermint essential oil. Mix well and divide salts into two separate bowls. Color one of the bowls of salts with drops of blue food coloring. Color the other bowl with drops of green food coloring. Using a funnel, transfer salts to a decorative sealable bottle, one color at a time, to make layers of blue and green salts. If desired, mix salts together before funneling into bottle.

Attach a gift tag with directions on how to use bath salts

Gift Tag Directions:

Soul Soothing Bath Salts

Add 2 to 4 tablespoons Soul Soothing Bath Salts to warm running bath water. Soak, relax and enjoy!

Soul Soothing Bath Salts

Add 2 to 4 tablespoons Soul Soothing Bath Salts to warm running bath water. Soak, relax and enjoy!

Soul Soothing Bath Salts

Add 2 to 4 tablespoons Soul Soothing Bath Salts to warm running bath water. Soak, relax and enjoy!

Soul Soothing Bath Salts

Add 2 to 4 tablespoons Soul Soothing Bath Salts to warm running bath water. Soak, relax and enjoy!

Soul Soothing Bath Salts

Add 2 to 4 tablespoons Soul Soothing Bath Salts to warm running bath water. Soak, relax and enjoy!

Herbal Bath Mix

1 C. oatmeal
1 T. dried herbs, use any from list below
1 drop essential oil, any kind

For a stimulating bath, use any of the following dried herbs: basil, bay, citronella, fennel, lavender, lemon verbena, marjoram, mint, sage, rosemary or thyme.

For a soothing bath, use any of the following dried herbs: chamomile, elder, primrose, jasmine, juniper berries, lemon balm, linden flowers, passionflower flowers, roses or violets.

In a blender, combine oatmeal and herbs, until evenly grated. Stir in essential oil. Using a funnel, transfer to a decorative sealable bottle.

Attach a gift tag with directions on how to use bath mix.

Gift Tag Directions:

Herbal Bath Mix

Add 2 to 4 tablespoons Herbal Bath Mix to warm running bath water. Soak, relax and enjoy!

Herbal Bath Mix

Add 2 to 4 tablespoons Herbal Bath Mix to warm running bath water. Soak, relax and enjoy!

Herbal Bath Mix

Add 2 to 4 tablespoons Herbal Bath Mix to warm running bath water. Soak, relax and enjoy!

Herbal Bath Mix

Add 2 to 4 tablespoons Herbal Bath Mix to warm running bath water. Soak, relax and enjoy!

Herbal Bath Mix

Add 2 to 4 tablespoons Herbal Bath Mix to warm running bath water. Soak, relax and enjoy!

Bubbling Jasmine Bath Salts

3 T. sea salts
3 T. baking soda
1 T. citric acid
8 drops jasmine essential oil

In a large jar with a lid, combine sea salts, baking soda, citric acid and jasmine essential oil. Cover jar and shake vigorously. Using a funnel, transfer to a decorative sealable bottle.

Attach a gift tag with directions on how to use bath salts.

Gift Tag Directions:

Bubbling Jasmine Bath Salts

Add 2 to 4 tablespoons Bubbling Jasmine Bath Salts to warm running bath water. Soak, relax and enjoy!

Bubbling Jasmine Bath Salts

Add 2 to 4 tablespoons Bubbling Jasmine Bath Salts to warm running bath water. Soak, relax and enjoy!

Bubbling Jasmine Bath Salts

Add 2 to 4 tablespoons Bubbling Jasmine Bath Salts to warm running bath water. Soak, relax and enjoy!

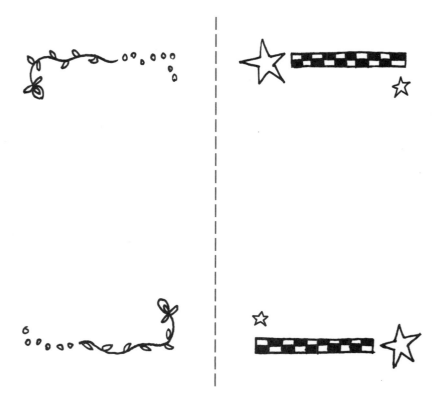

**Bubbling Jasmine
Bath Salts**

Add 2 to 4 tablespoons Bubbling Jasmine Bath Salts to warm running bath water. Soak, relax and enjoy!

**Bubbling Jasmine
Bath Salts**

Add 2 to 4 tablespoons Bubbling Jasmine Bath Salts to warm running bath water. Soak, relax and enjoy!

Citrus Fantasy Shower Gel

1/2 C. unscented shampoo
1/4 C. water
3/4 tsp. salt
15 drops citrus essential oil
Red and yellow food coloring

In a large bowl, combine shampoo and water. Mix until fully blended. Stir in salt and citrus essential oil. Mix in drops of red and yellow food coloring until shower gel is orange in color. Using a funnel, transfer to a decorative sealable bottle.

Attach a gift tag with directions on how to use shower gel.

Gift Tag Directions:

Citrus Fantasy Shower Gel

In a shower or bath, massage a generous amount of Citrus Fantasy Shower Gel gently into skin. Rinse clean with warm water.

**Citrus Fantasy
Shower Gel**

In a shower or bath, massage a generous amount of Citrus Fantasy Shower Gel gently into skin. Rinse clean with warm water.

**Citrus Fantasy
Shower Gel**

In a shower or bath, massage a generous amount of Citrus Fantasy Shower Gel gently into skin. Rinse clean with warm water.

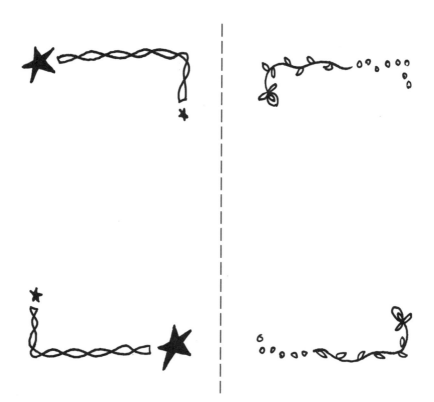

Citrus Fantasy Shower Gel

In a shower or bath, massage a generous amount of Citrus Fantasy Shower Gel gently into skin. Rinse clean with warm water.

Citrus Fantasy Shower Gel

In a shower or bath, massage a generous amount of Citrus Fantasy Shower Gel gently into skin. Rinse clean with warm water.

Foaming Vanilla Bath Soak

1 C. olive oil
1/2 C. liquid soap
1/4 C. honey
1 T. vanilla extract

In a medium bowl, combine olive oil, liquid soap, honey and vanilla. Mix well until thoroughly blended. Using a funnel, transfer to a decorative sealable bottle.

Attach a gift tag with directions on how to use bath soak.

Gift Tag Directions:

Foaming Vanilla Bath Soak

Shake bottle before using. Add 1/4 cup Foaming Vanilla Bath Soak to warm running bath water. Soak, relax and enjoy!

**Foaming Vanilla
Bath Soak**

Shake bottle
before using. Add
1/4 cup Foaming
Vanilla Bath Soak
to warm running
bath water. Soak,
relax and enjoy!

**Foaming Vanilla
Bath Soak**

Shake bottle
before using. Add
1/4 cup Foaming
Vanilla Bath Soak
to warm running
bath water. Soak,
relax and enjoy!

Foaming Vanilla Bath Soak

Shake bottle before using. Add 1/4 cup Foaming Vanilla Bath Soak to warm running bath water. Soak, relax and enjoy!

Foaming Vanilla Bath Soak

Shake bottle before using. Add 1/4 cup Foaming Vanilla Bath Soak to warm running bath water. Soak, relax and enjoy!

Tangerine Silky Smooth Lotion

1/4 C. lemon juice
1/4 C. glycerin
40 drops orange essential oil

In a jar with a lid, combine lemon juice, glycerin and orange essential oil. Cover jar and shake vigorously. Using a funnel, transfer to a small decorative sealable bottle.

Attach a gift tag with directions on how to use lotion.

Gift Tag Directions:

Tangerine Silky Smooth Lotion

Massage a small amount of Tangerine Silky Smooth Lotion into clean, dry skin for a smooth silky finish. A little goes a long way!

Tangerine Silky Smooth Lotion

Massage a small amount of Tangerine Silky Smooth Lotion into clean, dry skin for a smooth silky finish. A little goes a long way!

Tangerine Silky Smooth Lotion

Massage a small amount of Tangerine Silky Smooth Lotion into clean, dry skin for a smooth silky finish. A little goes a long way!

Tangerine Silky Smooth Lotion

Massage a small amount of Tangerine Silky Smooth Lotion into clean, dry skin for a smooth silky finish. A little goes a long way!

Tangerine Silky Smooth Lotion

Massage a small amount of Tangerine Silky Smooth Lotion into clean, dry skin for a smooth silky finish. A little goes a long way!

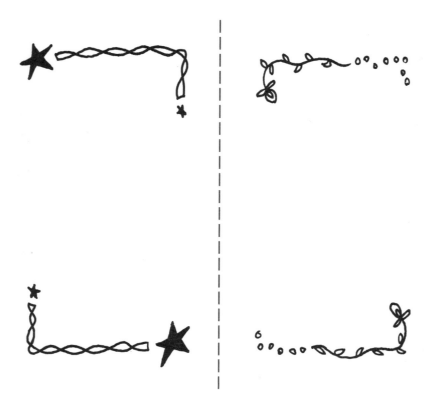

Peace of Mind Bath Salts

3/4 C. Epsom salts
1/4 C. sea salts
1/2 C. baking soda
2 T. cornstarch
5 drops peppermint essential oil
5 drops lavender essential oil
5 drops eucalyptus essential oil
5 drops rosemary essential oil
5 drops blue food coloring, optional

In a large bowl, combine Epsom salts, sea salts, baking soda and cornstarch by hand. Add essential oils, one drop at a time. If desired, mix in blue food coloring until evenly incorporated. Using a funnel, transfer to a decorative sealable bottle.

Attach a gift tag with directions on how to use bath salts.

Gift Tag Directions:

Peace of Mind Bath Salts

To relieve stress, add 1/4 cup Peace of Mind Bath Salts to warm running bath water. Soak, relax and enjoy!

**Peace of Mind
Bath Salts**

To relieve stress, add 1/4 cup Peace of Mind Bath Salts to warm running bath water. Soak, relax and enjoy!

**Peace of Mind
Bath Salts**

To relieve stress, add 1/4 cup Peace of Mind Bath Salts to warm running bath water. Soak, relax and enjoy!

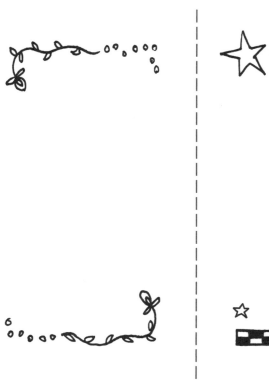

Peace of Mind Bath Salts

To relieve stress, add 1/4 cup Peace of Mind Bath Salts to warm running bath water. Soak, relax and enjoy!

Peace of Mind Bath Salts

To relieve stress, add 1/4 cup Peace of Mind Bath Salts to warm running bath water. Soak, relax and enjoy!

Lavender Moisturizing Bath Oil

1/2 C. avocado oil
40 drops lavender essential oil
Red and blue food coloring, optional

In a small bowl, combine avocado oil and lavender essential oil until well blended. If desired, add food coloring and mix until evenly incorporated. Using a funnel, transfer to a small decorative sealable bottle.

Attach a gift tag with directions on how to use bath oil.

Gift Tag Directions:

Lavender Moisturizing Bath Oil

Pour 2 to 4 tablespoons Lavender Moisturizing Bath Oil into warm running bath water. Soak, relax and enjoy!

**Lavender
Moisturizing Bath Oil**

Pour 2 to 4 tablespoons Lavender Moisturizing Bath Oil into warm running bath water. Soak, relax and enjoy!

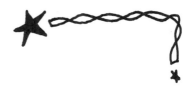

**Lavender
Moisturizing Bath Oil**

Pour 2 to 4 tablespoons Lavender Moisturizing Bath Oil into warm running bath water. Soak, relax and enjoy!

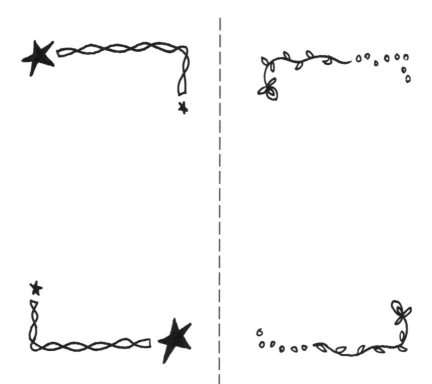

**Lavender
Moisturizing Bath Oil**

Pour 2 to 4 tablespoons Lavender Moisturizing Bath Oil into warm running bath water. Soak, relax and enjoy!

**Lavender
Moisturizing Bath Oil**

Pour 2 to 4 tablespoons Lavender Moisturizing Bath Oil into warm running bath water. Soak, relax and enjoy!

Orange Poppy Exfoliating Scrub

1/2 C. olive oil
1/2 C. poppy seeds
1/4 tsp. orange essential oil

In a medium bowl, combine olive oil, poppy seeds and orange essential oil. Mix until well blended. Using a funnel, transfer to a decorative sealable bottle.

Attach a gift tag with directions on how to use exfoliating scrub.

Gift Tag Directions:

Orange Poppy Exfoliating Scrub

In a shower or bath, massage a generous amount of Orange Poppy Exfoliating Scrub gently into hands, feet or dry skin. Leave on for a few minutes before rinsing clean with warm water.

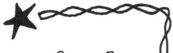

Orange Poppy Exfoliating Scrub

In a shower or bath, massage a generous amount of Orange Poppy Exfoliating Scrub gently into hands, feet or dry skin. Leave on for a few minutes before rinsing clean with warm water.

Orange Poppy Exfoliating Scrub

In a shower or bath, massage a generous amount of Orange Poppy Exfoliating Scrub gently into hands, feet or dry skin. Leave on for a few minutes before rinsing clean with warm water.

Orange Poppy Exfoliating Scrub

In a shower or bath, massage a generous amount of Orange Poppy Exfoliating Scrub gently into hands, feet or dry skin. Leave on for a few minutes before rinsing clean with warm water.

Orange Poppy Exfoliating Scrub

In a shower or bath, massage a generous amount of Orange Poppy Exfoliating Scrub gently into hands, feet or dry skin. Leave on for a few minutes before rinsing clean with warm water.

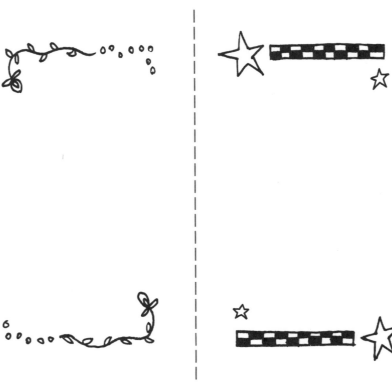

Dreamy Time Bath Salts

2 C. Epsom salts
1 C. sea salts
10 drops vanilla essential oil
Blue and red food coloring

In a large bowl, combine Epsom salts, sea salts and vanilla essential oil and mix well. Add drops of blue and red food coloring to make purple salts. Mix well. Using a funnel, transfer to a decorative sealable bottle.

Attach a gift tag with directions on how to use bath salts

Gift Tag Directions:

Dreamy Time Bath Salts

Add 2 to 4 tablespoons Dreamy Time Bath Salts to warm running bath water. Soak, relax and enjoy!

**Dreamy Time
Bath Salts**

Add 2 to 4 tablespoons Dreamy Time Bath Salts to warm running bath water. Soak, relax and enjoy!

**Dreamy Time
Bath Salts**

Add 2 to 4 tablespoons Dreamy Time Bath Salts to warm running bath water. Soak, relax and enjoy!

**Dreamy Time
Bath Salts**

Add 2 to 4 tablespoons Dreamy Time Bath Salts to warm running bath water. Soak, relax and enjoy!

**Dreamy Time
Bath Salts**

Add 2 to 4 tablespoons Dreamy Time Bath Salts to warm running bath water. Soak, relax and enjoy!

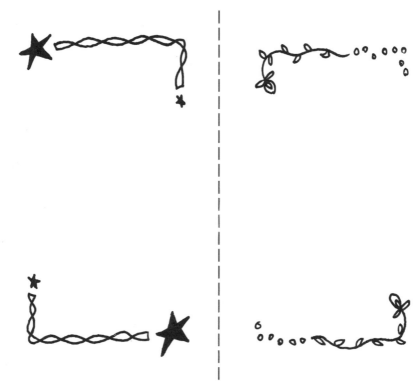

Glowing Skin Bath Oil

1 C. salt
1 C. vegetable oil
1 C. unscented liquid soap
10 drops vanilla essential oil
Food coloring, optional

In a medium bowl, combine salt, vegetable oil, unscented liquid soap and vanilla essential oil. Mix until well blended. If desired, add food coloring and mix until evenly incorporated. Using a funnel, transfer to a decorative sealable bottle.

Attach a gift tag with directions on how to use bath oil.

Gift Tag Directions:

Glowing Skin Bath Oil

Shake bottle before using. Pour 2 tablespoons Glowing Skin Bath Oil into warm running bath water. Soak, relax and enjoy! Or, rub bath oil into skin during shower and rinse.

Glowing Skin Bath Oil

Shake bottle before using. Pour 2 tablespoons Glowing Skin Bath Oil into warm running bath water. Soak, relax and enjoy! Or, rub bath oil into skin during shower and rinse.

Glowing Skin Bath Oil

Shake bottle before using. Pour 2 tablespoons Glowing Skin Bath Oil into warm running bath water. Soak, relax and enjoy! Or, rub bath oil into skin during shower and rinse.

Glowing Skin Bath Oil

Shake bottle before using. Pour 2 tablespoons Glowing Skin Bath Oil into warm running bath water. Soak, relax and enjoy! Or, rub bath oil into skin during shower and rinse.

Glowing Skin Bath Oil

Shake bottle before using. Pour 2 tablespoons Glowing Skin Bath Oil into warm running bath water. Soak, relax and enjoy! Or, rub bath oil into skin during shower and rinse.

Strawberry Shortcake Bubble Bath

1/2 C. unscented shampoo
3/4 C. water
1/2 tsp. salt
15 drops strawberry shortcake or
   cherry essential oil
Red food coloring

In a large bowl, pour shampoo and add water. Stir gently until well mixed. Add salt and stir until mixture thickens. Add strawberry shortcake or cherry essential oil and mix well. Add food coloring and mix until evenly incorporated. Using a funnel, transfer to a decorative sealable bottle.

Attach a gift tag with directions on how to use bubble bath.

Gift Tag Directions:

Strawberry Shortcake Bubble Bath

Add 2 to 4 tablespoons Strawberry Shortcake Bubble Bath to warm running bath water. Soak, relax and enjoy!

**Strawberry
Shortcake
Bubble Bath**

Add 2 to 4 tablespoons Strawberry Shortcake Bubble Bath to warm running bath water. Soak, relax and enjoy!

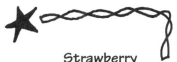

**Strawberry
Shortcake
Bubble Bath**

Add 2 to 4 tablespoons Strawberry Shortcake Bubble Bath to warm running bath water. Soak, relax and enjoy!

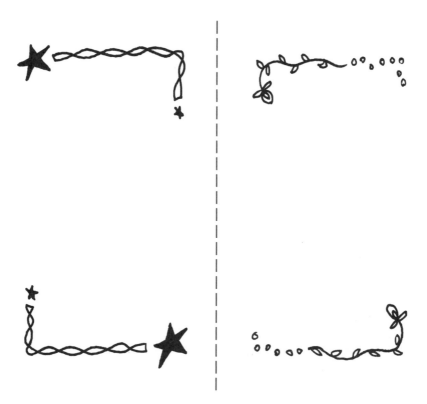

Strawberry Shortcake Bubble Bath

Add 2 to 4 tablespoons Strawberry Shortcake Bubble Bath to warm running bath water. Soak, relax and enjoy!

Strawberry Shortcake Bubble Bath

Add 2 to 4 tablespoons Strawberry Shortcake Bubble Bath to warm running bath water. Soak, relax and enjoy!

Energizing Citrus Bath Salts

2 C. Epsom salts
1 C. sea salts
15 drops citrus essential oil
Red and yellow food coloring

In a large bowl, combine Epsom salts, sea salts and citrus essential oil. Mix well and divide salts into two separate bowls. Color one of the bowls of salts with drops of red food coloring. Color the other bowl with drops of red and yellow food coloring to make orange salts. Using a funnel, transfer salts to a decorative sealable bottle, one color at a time, to make layers of red and orange salts. If desired, mix salts together before funneling into bottle.

Attach a gift tag with directions on how to use bath salts

Gift Tag Directions:

Energizing Citrus Bath Salts

Add 2 to 4 tablespoons Energizing Citrus Bath Salts to warm running bath water. Soak, relax and enjoy!

Energizing Citrus Bath Salts

Add 2 to 4 tablespoons Energizing Citrus Bath Salts to warm running bath water. Soak, relax and enjoy!

Energizing Citrus Bath Salts

Add 2 to 4 tablespoons Energizing Citrus Bath Salts to warm running bath water. Soak, relax and enjoy!

**Energizing Citrus
Bath Salts**

Add 2 to 4 tablespoons Energizing Citrus Bath Salts to warm running bath water. Soak, relax and enjoy!

**Energizing Citrus
Bath Salts**

Add 2 to 4 tablespoons Energizing Citrus Bath Salts to warm running bath water. Soak, relax and enjoy!

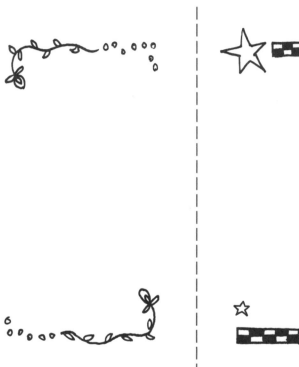

Index

Bubbling Jasmine Bath Salts	21
Citrus Fantasy Shower Gel	23
Dreamy Time Bath Salts	35
Energizing Citrus Bath Salts	41
Fairy Dust Glitter Gel	7
Foaming Vanilla Bath Soak	25
Glowing Skin Bath Oil	37
Grapefruit Bubble Bath	3
Herbal Bath Mix	19
Lavender Moisturizing Bath Oil	31
Lavender Dreams Bubble Bath	15
Muscle Relaxing Bath Salts	5
Oatmeal Milk Bath	11
Orange Poppy Exfoliating Scrub	33
Peace of Mind Bath Salts	29
Romantic Bath Crystals	1
Skin So Soft Bath Soak	9
Soothing Rose Bath Crystals	13
Soul Soothing Bath Salts	17
Strawberry Shortcake Bubble Bath	39
Tangerine Silky Smooth Lotion	27

Recipes Shown on Front Cover

From left to right

Strawberry Shortcake Bubble Bath 39

Lavender Dreams Bubble Bath 15

Energizing Citrus Bath Salts 41

Oatmeal Milk Bath 11

To purchase more books by **CQ Products** see your local gift or craft store!

Or call to order a FREE catalog at 866-804-9892

507 Industrial St.
Waverly, IA 50677

www.cqproducts.com • fax 800-886-7496